GREENHOUSE GARDENING FOR BEGINNERS

A COMPLETE ILLUSTRATED GUIDE TO START GROWING FRUITS AND VEGETABLES ALL YEAR-ROUND AND HOW TO BUILD YOUR OWN DIY GREENHOUSE

GORDON GREEN.

Table of Contents

Introduction 1
Chapter 1 Different Types Of Greenhouses 11
    Lean-to Greenhouse Structure 13
    Even Span Greenhouse Structure 15
    Uneven Span Greenhouse Structure 16
    A-Frame Greenhouse Structure 18
    Quonset Greenhouse Structure/ Hoop-House Structure 20
    Gothic Arch Greenhouse Structure 22
    Ridge and Furrow Greenhouse Structure 23
    Sawtooth Greenhouse Structure 25
    Cold Frame Greenhouse Structure 26
    Hotbed Greenhouse 27
    Window Farm 28
Chapter 2 Constructing Your DIY Greenhouse 29
Chapter 3 Greenhouse Climate Control 39
Chapter 4 Start Growing In Your Greenhouse 51
Chapter 5 Managing And Operating A Greenhouse 64
Chapter 6 Insect, Pest And Mite Management 69
Chapter 7 Fertilizers And Agrochemicals 81
Chapter 8 Hydroponics In A Greenhouse 87
Chapter 9 Making A Profit From Your Greenhouse 91
Chapter 10 Year-Round Growing 95
Chapter 11 Planting in Warm and Cold Weather 104
Chapter 12 The Cost Factor 108
Chapter 13 Common Mistakes and How to Avoid Them ... 111
Conclusion 118

Introduction

Greenhouse gardening is not a modern concept. The technology and system dates back to the Roman Empire. Earliest reference to the greenhouse gardening concept is directed to the Roman Emperor Tiberius. He demanded to have Armenian cucumbers every day at the royal table. Royal gardeners thought of ways to obey the emperor's order. They found out that by creating a sealed enclosure, they can control temperatures, humidity and light exposure required by cucumbers for growth and fruit bearing. They used a special system very similar to that of the modern greenhouses. The first modern greenhouse, with a more refined system than what the Romans used, was made in Italy in the 13th century.

During those times, having a greenhouse was limited to the wealthy. By the 19th century, greenhouses became more of an academic need. Universities put up large greenhouses, designed to hold several rare species of plants. During this time, the Western civilization was starting to explore the other side of the world. Explorers and scholars were bringing back a lot of specimen from these exotic places, most of which were pretty interesting, but cannot tolerate cold climates. In order to preserve the plants in their full, natural bloom, greenhouses were the likely solution.

Greenhouse gardening can then be defined as the science of growing plants in an erected building with materials usually transparent or translucent such that the plants are provided with controlled favorable environmental conditions. The technology involved in greenhouse gardening makes it possible to grow any kind of plant whether in season or out of season as long as an effort is being made to supply the plant with the necessary environmental conditions. An attractive attribute of this technique is that it is most cost-effective as it is affordable for almost all home growers. However, care needs to be taken and enough knowledge about this concept should be gathered because ignorance on the part of the grower can result in the complete loss of the entire plantation. Greenhouses ensure adequate growing temperature condition for the plants all year round and when the system is used on a large scale, there are advanced technological tools that are specially designed to enhance grow lights supply, and subsequently improve the productivity. Plants that are cultivated in greenhouses receive protection against conditions like soil erosion, harsh weather, violent rain and storm, plant pathogens, etc. This system of gardening is also called glasshouse or hothouse by some growers, and the major reason for setting it up is arguably so as to secure a considerable quantity of water vapor and heat in order to maintain humidity and proper temperature in the greenhouse.

The technology of greenhouse gardening serves as a viable solution to bridge the gap between the increasing world population and the increasing demand. The gap was created as a result of the urbanization of certain countries involving the construction of roads, etc. and also industrialization which has unavoidably rendered many arable lands non-arable. The concept of the greenhouse technique is simply growing plants within a confined space under a controlled favorable environmental condition, that is, the conditions necessary for the growth of the cultivated plants are provided within the confined space regardless of the climate or season.

The growth of plants under adverse weather conditions will eventually become stunted, this is why plants grow better in a greenhouse although, the growth of plants in the greenhouse is influenced by humidity, ventilation, light and also the rate of plant watering. The environmental condition of the greenhouse can be classified into physical environment – which include water, light, temperature, etc. and the biotic environment – which include insects, microorganisms, etc. Humidity level above 85% in the greenhouse should, by all means, be avoided as this tends to cause more harm than good to the plants. When the humidity level in the greenhouse is too much, the plants become weak and flaccid in which case the humid air needs to be exhausted. The need for the presence of fresh air in the greenhouse cannot be overemphasized as it encourages photosynthesis, pollination and pest prevention. Plants generally require about 6 to 12 hours of light daily, therefore, in a situation where the plants in the greenhouse are not exposed to enough natural light, artificial light should be incorporated and adequately so. Also, too much supply of water in the greenhouse is just as dangerous to the plants as the lack of water supply. But factors such as growing medium, temperature, plant size, etc. contribute greatly to the determination of the amount of watering required by the plant. After you have selected the location to set up your greenhouse, the building can be self-built by placing an order for an already made 'do- it- yourself' greenhouse kit. Setting things up in most cases is simple but in some other cases, it can also be a bit complex. For starters, not much high-tech equipment is required in order to practice greenhouse gardening. The greenhouse technique can be practiced simply or expanded depending on the scale of production intended.

How do greenhouses work?

A greenhouse is designed to keep heat inside the building. It allows sunlight to enter and warm the inside of the building. The structure is insulated, which prevents heat from escaping.

Most parts of the greenhouse are made from clear plastic or glass because these materials allow more natural sunlight to pass through. Sunlight is the main source of thermal energy, as well as a crucial source of energy for plant photosynthesis. In addition, it warms up the ground and the air inside the greenhouse. The sun-warmed ground provides additional heating long after the sun goes down. The insulation system keeps this heat within the structure to maintain the desired temperatures.

Purposes of a Greenhouse

Modern uses of greenhouses include shielding plants from the extremes of temperatures that may damage them. It makes it possible to grow plants during the cold months to sustain a steady supply of fresh food. Seasonal fruits can be enjoyed year-round. A greenhouse can be made to simulate the growing conditions of a particular fruit, even if the outside weather is totally different. Summer fruits can be enjoyed in the winter. Tropical fruits can be served in the homes of those in the Northern hemisphere.

Greenhouse gardening extends the growing season of valuable crops like tomatoes and corn. The controlled environment allows for better crop yield. Changing weather can often devastate crops, but not so if grown within a greenhouse. Flowers can be grown all year-round, too. Horticulture fans and flower lovers can cultivate flowers that do not grow naturally in their areas. Cold northern places can very well grow tropical flowers within greenhouses. Rare orchids can be cultivated in colder areas. All these thanks to greenhouses.

BENEFITS OF A GREENHOUSE

Plants can be majorly cultivated using three different systems of cultivation; these are the in-ground system, greenhouse system, or hydroponic system of cultivation. While there is no technicality involved in the in-ground system, the greenhouse and hydroponic system both have certain advantages over the in-ground system. Virtually any kind of plant can be cultivated in a greenhouse, but with careful selection of the plants to be grown, profit can be maximized. There are certain times of the year when the weather becomes unsuitable for plant growth; there are times it becomes too windy, too dark, too cold, too hot, or too rainy and it takes a miracle for plants especially vegetables to survive such climatic condition. Greenhouse growers have no headache whenever the climatic condition becomes adverse because it has always been their responsibility to control the environmental condition in their greenhouse garden.

1. Out of season Production

This is perhaps the major reason many growers dabble into this system of gardening. Greenhouse gardening offers you the benefit of a longer growing season, that is, plants can be grown all year round in a greenhouse. When 'out of season' crops are made available, there is usually a huge rise in their selling prices when there is high market demand and it consequently yields a high-profit return on the investment made. However, it is important to keep in mind that not all 'out of season' crops have high market demand. Therefore, it is necessary that you carry out adequate research about the plant to be cultivated before investing in its 'out of season' production. Some growers call this stage the preliminary research stage, it is to ensure that the investment you are about to make will be profitable at the end of the day. In greenhouse gardening, the plants grow faster and healthier and therefore can be made available early before their season, during their season and also when they are out of season. The extended growing season is one of the major benefits derived from greenhouse gardening.

2. Higher Yield

When the greenhouse system of gardening is compared to the traditional open-field cultivation, the yield from a greenhouse is usually 10 times higher in quantity and quality. Although this depends on the size of a greenhouse used, also the type of plant being cultivated and the environmental condition provided in the greenhouse if optimum. The plants in a greenhouse usually have little or no enemy such as plant diseases to fight against and so it is easy for them to grow healthily and germinate quickly. The favorable environmental condition that plants enjoy in the greenhouse is a stimulant for healthy growth and higher yield. This particular benefit from using a greenhouse is being utilized in many countries of the world where the population is constantly on the increase in order to ensure that there is enough food in circulation that will meet the need of the teeming population.

3. Higher Quality

Another benefit that is derived from using a greenhouse system is that it gives quality yield at the end of each growing season. As stated earlier that the yield from a greenhouse is usually 10 times higher than open field cultivation in quantity and also in quality. Using a greenhouse for your plant cultivation will not only offer you the benefit of producing more yield from your cultivation, but you can also be assured that the product you will obtain will be of great quality. Higher yield and higher quality are benefits enjoyed by practicing greenhouse gardening.

4. Plant/Crop Reliability

Due to the absence of pests, diseases and other plant infections in a greenhouse, the plants cultivated in the greenhouse have increased reliability. That is, there is a reduced risk of infection and the yield from the greenhouse cultivation can be trusted as clean & healthy. Also, unlike conventional gardening, the grower remains unbothered during adverse climatic conditions because the plants in the greenhouse are totally not affected by the external bad weather. The reliability of plant healthy growth is high in a greenhouse system.

5. Pest and disease-free production

A greenhouse makes it easy to protect the plants being cultivated from pest attack and keep them free from diseases. A good and strong greenhouse should, however, be purchased in order to easily achieve this and keep pests away from the plants. The protection provided by the greenhouse is another great benefit that gives the plants cultivated through this method an edge over the plants cultivated using the conventional an open field.

6. Provides the plants with optimum growing condition

This is another benefit that plants in a greenhouse enjoy as they are provided with the optimum growing condition and therefore, they grow faster, better and healthier. Providing the best growing environment for your plants is a jackpot that harnesses the highest possible growth rate of the plants. Regardless of the plants being cultivated, the greenhouse provides the grower with the opportunity to supply the plants with a favorable and optimum growing environment. This growing environment can sometimes mean trapping beneficial insects inside the greenhouse because not all insects are harmful to the plants. Some are very beneficial and while these beneficial insects can come and go as they like in an open field system, an advantage of using a greenhouse is that they can be trapped inside and therefore continuously enhance the growth of the plants in the greenhouse.

7. Absence of toxic pesticides

In the traditional system of gardening, there is sometimes the need for the strong application of toxic pesticides in order to fight against certain pest attacks. These toxic pesticides, no matter how little, usually reflect on the yield at the end of the day but the good news is that there is usually no need for such application of pesticides in a greenhouse. This keeps the plants in the greenhouse fresh and also ensures clean yield at the end of the growing season. This benefit also makes it possible to produce genetically superior transplants.

8. Energy-saving and less labor-intensive

In a greenhouse, the application of water, light, nutrient, etc. is totally controlled by the grower. This makes it easy to control how they are supplied unlike in conventional gardening where it is more difficult to conserve energy. The ability to conserve energy in a greenhouse helps to improve the environment at large. Greenhouse gardening also makes gardening an interesting thing to do. It makes gardening less labor-intensive and almost completely stress-free. This realization is perhaps the reason we have more home growers lately as many growers practice greenhouse gardening just for the fun of it or better still as a hobby.

Other benefits of using a greenhouse include the efficient utilization of nutrients, water, pesticide (if any), and also the bridging of gap in plant cultivation that exist as a result of bad climatic conditions and the presence of non-arable lands in most areas.

Chapter 1 Different Types Of Greenhouses

The type of greenhouse structure determines the productivity and efficiency of your gardening activities. New to greenhouse gardening. It will make it easier for beginners to choose the right structure based on their needs.

As a plant grower, you need to understand the efficiency of plant production and control of environmental conditions. Choosing the right greenhouse will enable you to create an ideal working environment for your vegetables, herbs, and fruits. It also allows you to create a plant growing plan that ensures you meet the specific needs of your crop.

These designs are based on the materials, shape, utility, and construction process. Most designs are classified as:

Attached

- Lean-to greenhouse structure
- Even span greenhouse structure

Freestanding or independent structures

- Uneven span greenhouse structure
- A-frame greenhouse structure

- Quonset greenhouse structure

- Gothic arch greenhouse structure

Gutter connected structures

- Ridge and furrow type greenhouse

- Sawtooth greenhouse

Lean-to Greenhouse Structure

Just like the name suggests, a lean-to greenhouse structure is built leaning on the side of another structure. It is classified as an attached greenhouse structure, meaning that the roof of the greenhouse connects to another building. You don't have to build all the four walls of the greenhouse because, by design, it shares one of its walls.

The structure should face the right direction to obtain adequate sunlight exposure. It should mostly face the southern side and the roof should have the best covering material. a lean-to greenhouse is ideal for growing herbs and vegetables.

This structure was common during the Victorian period, and it is one of the traditional structures available. Building against the wall offers additional support to the structure, making it strong and wind resistant. The wall also absorbs heat during the day and releases that heat at night, which helps to maintain the temperature of the greenhouse during the cool nights.

If you're planning to use lean-to structure, you need to put the height of the structure into consideration together with any metal base. This ensures the ridges do not come in contact with any windows or drainage pipes in the principal building.

Advantages

- Cost-effective: This type of structure is less expensive compared to other greenhouse structures.

- Minimize building materials: The design is built against an existing wall, thus saving you on building material for four walls. It also minimizes roofing material requirements, since the design makes the best use of sunlight.

- The structure is constructed close to water, electricity, and heat.

Disadvantages

- Limited sunlight: Building lean-to structure against a house or garage limits the amount of sunlight to only the three walls. It will also have limited light, ventilation, and minimum temperature control.

- Limited to the building orientation: The best structure should be on the southern exposure. The height of the building or the supporting wall affects the design and the size of the greenhouse.

- Temperature control: It is difficult to control the temperature of the structure because the wall absorbs a lot of heat during the day and distributes it for use in the cool nights. Some translucent covers lose heat more rapidly, making it difficult to control the heat.

- Foundation: You need to build a strong foundation for this greenhouse to last long, especially when using glass with the lean-to greenhouse.

Even Span Greenhouse Structure

Even span is another attached type of greenhouse, and it attaches more to promote plant growth. This standard structure is attached to a building, and its roof is made of two slopes of equal length and width. The structure can allow you to plant two to three rows, with two side benches and a wide bench at the center.

Even span design is more flexible and has curved eaves to boost their shape. Due to its great shape, there is plenty of air circulation in the greenhouse, thus making it easier to control temperatures. You also need to have an extra heating system especially when the structure is far away from a heated building. The heating system is especially important during the winter season.

Advantages

- It provides enough space for the growth of plants and vegetables.
- It is easier and more economic in construction, making it the most popular design for a greenhouse.
- You have easy access to water and electricity within the building.

Disadvantages

- High cost of construction and heating system compared to the lean-to structure.
- Reduced sunlight exposure due to the shadow from the house it is attached to.

Uneven Span Greenhouse Structure

Uneven-span greenhouse structure
Photo credit pinterest

In this structure, the roof is made of uneven or unequal width. The greenhouse is constructed such that one rooftop slope is longer than the other, making the design suitable for a hilly terrain or when you want to take advantage of solar energy.

Uneven slopes are laid so the steeper angles of the greenhouse face to the south.

Uneven greenhouses are no longer used because most farmers prefer setting up a greenhouse on a flat land.

Advantages

- As mentioned, this greenhouse is in a hilly areas.

- There is no obstruction of sunlight because the longer slope allows for more sunlight to enter the structure. The longer side also faces south, thus maximizing heat from the sun's rays.

Disadvantages

- It can be costly compared to even span greenhouses.
- They require more support on the slanted roof.
- Uneven span greenhouses usually need a lot of maintenance on the roof after some time.
- Too much solar can penetrate to the greenhouse if the uneven-span greenhouse is located in areas close to the equator.

A-Frame Greenhouse Structure

The A-frame greenhouse style is one of the most common designs. The structure is simple to set and it is ideal for a small backyard garden. To form the A-frame, you would attach the roof and sidewalls of greenhouse together, which forms a triangular-like shape.

Most of A-framed greenhouses use translucent, poly-carbonate material, which helps to eliminate the cost from having to buy glass material. Most A-framed greenhouses are laid down in an open field or at the backyard facing the southern side.

Advantages

- It maximizes on the use of space along the side walls.
- Simple and straightforward to construct.
- Conservative structure style, using minimal material

Disadvantages

- It has poor air circulation at the corners of the triangle.
- Its narrow side walls limit the overall use of the greenhouse.

Quonset Greenhouse Structure/ Hoop-House Structure

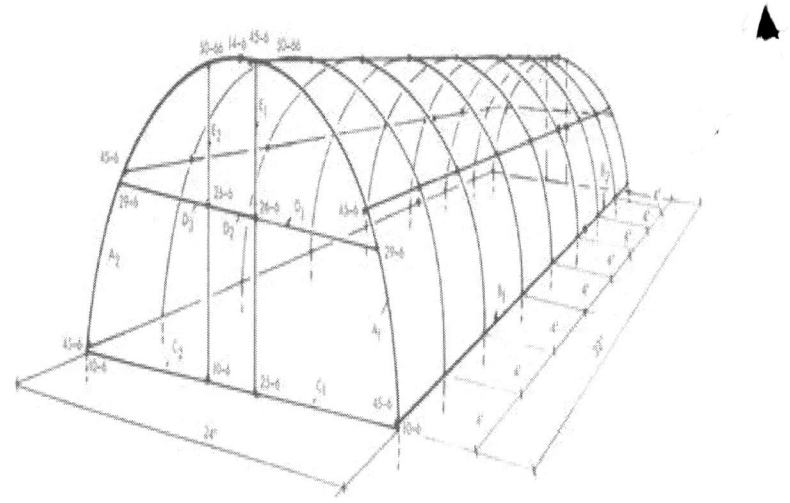

The quonset design has a curved roof or arched rafters, and its design is similar to military-hut style. The circular band in the structure's style is made of aluminum or PVC pipes, while the rooftop is made of plastic sheeting. The sidewalls of the design are set low, however, so there is not a whole lot of headroom. The hoops on the rooftop ensure there is no accumulation of snow and water on the top.

You would build this type of greenhouse in an open field or backyard with the structure facing the southern side.

Advantages

- Easy to build and one of the cheapest designs due to the use of plastic sheeting.

- Its design allows rain water and melted snow to run off.
- Suitable for a small plant growing space.

Disadvantages
- Limited storage space.
- Its frame design is not as sturdy as A-frame design.
- As stated, there is less headroom in the structure.

Gothic Arch Greenhouse Structure

Gothic arch has a nice aesthetic, and is one of the most visually pleasing designs available. The walls of the structure are bent over a frame, forming a pointed roof-like structure. The design requires less material to construct, as there is no need for trusses. Most of Gothic arch designs are made of plastic sheeting, and its design allows you to construct a large greenhouse where you can plant various products in rows.

Advantages

- The design has minimum heat exposure, thus making it easy to conserve heat.
- Plastic sheeting reduces the cost of construction.
- It has a simple and efficient design that allows rainwater and snow to flow away.

Disadvantages

- Not enough headroom and the design has a low sidewall height, which limits the storage of the greenhouse design.

Ridge and Furrow Greenhouse Structure

This type of design uses two or more A-framed design structures connected to one another along the roof eave length. The eaves offer more protection and act as a furrow to allow melted snow or rain water to flow away.

There are no side walls on the structure, which creates more ventilation in the greenhouse. It also reduces automation cost and fuel consumption, since only small wall area is exposed where the heat can escape.

Ridge and furrow greenhouse structure is ideal for growing vegetables, and they're mostly used in Europe, Canada, the Netherlands, and Scandinavian countries.

Advantages

- Ideal for large scale farming, and it's easy to expand this type of greenhouse.
- Provides more ventilation into the greenhouse.

- Requires few materials for construction because of its lack of side walls.
- Requires little energy to cool and heat.

Disadvantages
- Lack of proper water drainage system will damage your plants.
- Although the design has no side walls, shadows from the gutters can prevent sunlight from entering the greenhouse.

Sawtooth Greenhouse Structure

This type of greenhouse structure is similar to the ridge and furrow; however, sawtooth offers more natural ventilation. This is due to its natural ventilation flow path developed as a result of the sawtooth design. The roof provides 25% of the total ventilation to the greenhouse, and opening the sawtooth vents will ensure there is continuous airflow into the greenhouse. This makes it easy to control the temperatures and ensure the plants are in good climatic conditions for their growth.

Advantages
- Sawtooth arches provide excellent light transmission into the greenhouse.
- High rooftop allows for natural heat ventilation and airflow in the greenhouse.
- Excellent structure for both warm and cold climatic conditions.
- Simple and strong greenhouse structure.
- Has a large farming area.

Cold Frame Greenhouse Structure

Cold frame is ideal for greenhouse gardening in your backyard, and allows you to plant plants and vegetables at any time. It is one of the cheapest and simplest greenhouses you can set up. In cold frame gardening, you place a glass or plastic sheeting as the cover of the greenhouse structure, which will help in protecting your crops from frost, snow, rain, wind, or low temperatures.

Cold-frame greenhouse is suitable for planting cold-loving plants like broccoli, cauliflower, and cabbage among others.

Based on your budget, you can go for glass, polycarbonate, or plastic sheeting material to construct the greenhouse. The design requires a few openings to allow ventilation of heat into the greenhouse.

Advantages

- Simple design and easy to manage.

- Made from old windows or old wood pallets, which minimizes the cost of construction.

Disadvantages

- Overheating problem—a single day with a lot of sun and closed windows can do a lot of damage to the plants.

- Recycling of the old materials can affect the material quality of the greenhouse.

Hotbed Greenhouse

The hotbed structure acts as a miniature type of greenhouse that traps heat from solar radiation. This greenhouse can provide a favorable environment for plants that need a lot of heat like tomatoes, eggplants, and peppers.

If you want to extend the growing season, you can use hotbeds to provide the right weather conditions for your crops. Whether during winter, summer, or spring, there is always a family of vegetables, fruits, or herbs you can grow.

The hotbed structure provides a heat source to the crops through manure rather than using heat source from electricity, helping to speed up the growth of your plants.

When using a hotbed, you can set up the garden as wide as you want, provided the ratio of manure used and the growing medium is 3:1. The amount of time and money you invest in the garden will determine your farm produce success.

Advantages
- Simple to design.
- Inexpensive.

Disadvantages
- Hotbeds only lasts two months, so you will need to remove and replace the material with new ones around that time.

Window Farm

A window farm is an indoor farming garden for most vegetables. In a window farm, plants rely on the natural light from the window and temperature control from your living area to grow. This method is ideal for those who don't have a backyard or enough space to construct a standalone greenhouse.

You should set the structure in a window where it can receive a lot of light, facing toward the south.

Advantages

- Amazing for growing vegetables.
- Simple design and easy to construct.

Disadvantages

- Requires more components like nutrients, tubes, and pumps to grow your vegetables.
- It is difficult to maintain compared to a normal, soil-based greenhouse.

Chapter 2 Constructing Your DIY Greenhouse

Greenhouses are not that hard to build. You can also get greenhouse kits from stores or even buy a greenhouse by yourself.

3. Start by choosing a location. Greenhouses require lots of sunlight. Choose a spot that gives you adequate sunlight. This is usually found on the southern side of any garden or farmland. It is important to choose the spot that gives maximum morning sun and is not obstructed by tall plants or trees. This will reduce the amount of sunlight that the greenhouse will receive. Another important thing to remember while choosing the spot for the greenhouse is the other structures in the periphery of the greenhouse. All of these structures are best located on the northern side of the garden or farmland.

4. Measure your location using a tape and remember the bigger your greenhouse is, the more money you will require to make it. If you have little to no experience in building things, then it is best to get a greenhouse kit that will give you all the materials that you will require.

5. The best locations are the ones that are constructed with one wall that is already built. In this way, you can use this one wall to construct the remaining portion of your greenhouse. Also,

if the wall is that of your house, the warmth will be an additional boost to the plants in the greenhouse. Support this structure with wooden beams or steel beams or rebar.

6. Build a frame using the support structures as a guide. The easiest is to create a dome-shaped greenhouse. However, the problem is the lack of space inside. Create and build frames using steel beams and connect these dome beams using steel rods or wooden rods. It is very important to choose a sturdy and rigid frame. It is best to seek architectural help to prevent the frames from toppling over.

7. Once the skeletal system for the greenhouse is built you can start by choosing the material you want over the greenhouse. Unless you are a professional who has had lots of prior experience, it is best to stick with a cover that is sturdy and functional. Specialized plastic and covers like UV stabilized polyethylene are good alternate sources. They are durable, light, and inexpensive. They also allow a good quantity of light transmission. The downside is that they need replacement and require washing as they accumulate dust and won't be as effective as glass. Alternately you can use a double walled plastic called polycarbonate or fiberglass, which are slightly more expensive materials but still excellent alternates.

8. Connect the entire area with dowels and a good hardy wire and place stakes on the ground. Add a layer of rebar for additional reinforcement. You can also add PVC if you want.

9. Once the PVC and rebar set, pour a good quantity of gravel inside the boundaries. This will act as a drainage for the plants and will absorb excess water, keeping the soil moist. It is also advisable to pour concrete on the floor of the greenhouse.

10. Get good quality wood and ensure you treat it to avoid degradation and depreciation. Cut and mold to fill the ground of the greenhouse by accounting for the way you want the plants to be arranged and the area available for plants, and to build any segregating units.

11. It is best to use metal dowels to keep the wooden drafts and segregation around. This will strengthen the pieces and account for less wear and tear and damage.

12. Seal the covering to the frame and ensure this is done as close to the frame as possible. You can tape and nail the material of the cover to the wooden frame. But take note to not stretch the material too much as this could tear the material. It is advisable to take your time doing this step.

13. Next comes the plan to control the environment of the greenhouse. Get heaters and fans to generate heat during the entire winter seasons. Place them in four corners in a diagonal position to account for optimal heating. Be sure to run these the entire winter to allow the plants to get the required warmth. It is also a good idea to install vents on the roof of the greenhouse, if this is not possible, build windows at the upper side of the walls to prevent the air from getting

stale inside and to also prevent excess heat. These vents will also allow you to reduce the amount of carbon dioxide inside the greenhouse.

14. Install perforated pipes along the areas where the plants are going to be cultivated inside the greenhouse. This will account for good irrigation. You can also construct the cultivable area of the land in a raised sloping platform to prevent excess water retention. It is also a good idea to have a couple of thermometers to measure the temperature of the environment inside the greenhouse and planting those plants, which are suitable for that particular temperature.

Common Greenhouse Accessories

It is important to remember that other than construction of the greenhouse, there are a number of accessories you may need to add to it.

- Automatic Louvers

The greenhouse design will mostly include opening vents, essential for controlling heat internally, but there are also solar-powered louvers that are automatic. These will allow you as the gardener to have a life outside of the greenhouse. You don't need to constantly keep monitoring the temperatures.

The louvers heat and shut as per the heating levels, and give an assurance that the plants will not be lost to overheating.

- Automatic Irrigation Systems

Seedlings die in most cases because you forgot to water them on time. The drip-irrigation systems, i.e. a hose with holes, can be set with a battery timer, to control the irrigation and watering of the plants. This is also ideal in ensuring you are not always present at the greenhouse.

- Greenhouse Shade Cloth

This is a cloth that is draped over the greenhouse to control and regulate the temperature inside. The best are UV stabilized cloths that have brass grommets and are available in many different densities. You can also choose to use split bamboo blinds.

The shade cloth should be secured on top of the greenhouse, and installed in an easy way allowing them to be drawn back during the mornings or evenings as needed.

- Hand-Watering Wands

A very strong water spray can easily flatten the small plants that are sprouting. The watering wands that have adjustable nozzles are designed to control the amount of water the plants receive. They also deliver water without disturbing the tender sprouts or soil around them.

- Potting Bench

These are containers that will hold the soil and allow you to grow your own seeds from start.

With all of the basic prerequisites gotten out of the way we can now get to the fun stuff—building your own greenhouse! Feel free to try them all for yourself!

Cold Frame Greenhouse

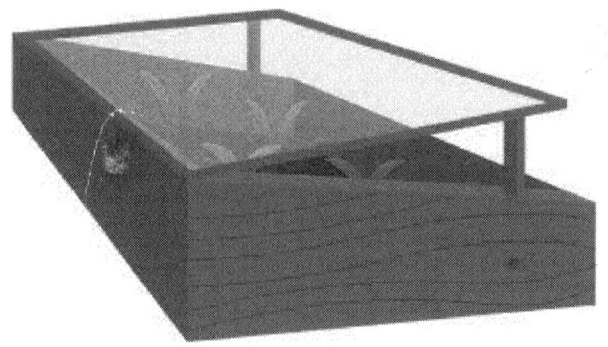

As the name just might imply, the Cold Frame Greenhouse is tailor made for colder environments. With a good cold frame construct you can keep those veggies growing well into the winter months. And the design of this apparatus could not be easier. At the most basic level a Cold Frame Greenhouse consists of a box frame and some sort of see-through lid stretched across the box. The box is typically made of wood, but in some cases even just cardboard could suffice. The clear lid of course is the point from which the sunlight can access the vegetation growing below.

The easiest way to create your own Cold Frame Greenhouse take four 4 by 4 boards and arrange them in a perfect square. Nail or screw the boards together so that they make up a complete assembly. Next take a sheet of plastic and using masking tape, tape it over the top of the wooden frame.

Now you can place this Cold Frame Greenhouse and place it over any piece of open ground from which you wish to grow your plants. Here this simple frame will serve its dual purpose of protecting and directing sunlight onto your growing fruits and veggies. This project is great for beginners because of its sheer simplicity, but it is also a good side project for veteran enthusiasts as well.

Window-Mounted Greenhouse

The windows of our home look out upon the sun and absorb its rays on a daily basis so it is only natural to look to these structures as a potential platform for our green house. So how can you do it? First off, you need to measure your window so that you can build your Window Mounted Greenhouse accordingly. The first thing that you need to keep in mind is the fact that the frame of your Window Mounted Greenhouse needs to be just a little bit narrower than your window frame so that it can fit inside.

This is the same kind of standard that window AC units use—the idea is to create the frame to be just slightly smaller so that it can fit right inside the existing window frame. With this structure in place you can then place tarp or glass over the frame. Hold the tarp in place with masking tape or some similar strong utility tape. Now simply set your veggies on the window sill of your Window Mounted Greenhouse and you are good to go—and your veggies are free to grow!

The Freestanding Greenhouse

The Freestanding Greenhouse is a structure that can be built outside and completely detached from the home. To get started take four 4 x 4s and stand them up to form a square—these are your corner posts. Now use additional 2 x 4s to fill in the spaces between. Next use additional 2 by 4's to create a triangular wooden frame for a roof. Drape clear plastic tarp over this structure to allow sunlight. You should have what looks like a see-through dome on top. After you have done all of this your Freestanding Greenhouse is complete.

Keeping Wind Out of Your Greenhouse

When the wind gets inside a greenhouse, it will put forth a valiant effort to constrain its way retreat once more. It seldom leaves a similar way it came in. As more air is diverted in the weight develops until something needs to give. Coating cuts fly off, and sheets are blown outwards. The most obvious route for the wind to pick up passage is through a missing sheet of glass, so supplant any that have just been smothered when you can. Most great coating organizations keep standard sizes of green glass in stock, however on the off chance that you have surprising sizes or need toughened glass or polycarbonate, at that point you may need to arrange it. The broken coating can be incidentally fixed with coating fix tape be that as it may, once more, it's ideal for supplanting it as quickly as time permits as the fix could come up short during further high winds or under day off.

At the point when I introduced my new glass sheets, I got severe about W-cuts (the ones that hold the glass into the frame) all round; the number of clasps that initially accompanied the greenhouse was not even close to enough! Silicone sealant can be utilized to verify the coating cuts set up for extra quality. A few greenhouses can be fitted with bar tops to hold the sheets in. These appear to be the most secure alternative, so it merits checking on the off chance that they're accessible for your model. Shockingly they're not made for my greenhouse, so all things being equal, I taped each pair of covering sheets together with coating fix tape, all around, as this appeared to be the weak point.

Wind can sneak in through the smallest of holes in a frame, so it's essential to obstruct. On the off chance that you look cautiously, you may find that the structure doesn't meet superbly at the corners or at either end of the edge. I utilized tape all around to cover the openings since that is the thing that I had convenient. However, silicone sealant would be a progressively perpetual arrangement. On the off chance that your greenhouse entryway has a lock or catch, ensure it holds the entryway safely shut. Something else, a substantial block wedged against it, should prevent it from blowing open.

Ensure any elastic coating strips and seals around the entryway, windows and different vents are in excellent condition, and supplant if essential. Windows and vents should close cosily. I have discovered that staying a segment of foam against hotspot tape (expected for loop house use) around the frame of my greenhouse's rooftop window vent gives it a significantly improved seal and stops it shaking in the wind. Sometimes an entire greenhouse can get airborne, notably lighter ones with polycarbonate coating. Stay away from this by ensuring that it's all around moored down. Mine is dashed to a metal base, which sits on soil yet is profoundly cemented in at each corner. It has never moved.

We absorb carbon dioxide as the plants grow and produce oxygen. But many people do not know that oxygen is required for plants to grow. Their roots require oxygen from the fresh air. The roots need oxygen to expand, and this is directly related to the ability of the plant to take nutrients from the soil.

Proper ventilation can keep fresh air flowing in the inside of your greenhouse so your plants can survive. Healthy plants are going to grow faster and give you the best fruit yield.

Maintaining the proper airflow in your greenhouse will take expert knowledge on how to do this. The type of ventilation system that you choose to use will depend on your greenhouse design and the plants that you grow. Some of them are human, some of them are mechanical.

Ventilation of the natural system can only involve opening up a part of the greenhouse. The greenhouse design of the hoop is perfect for this. A mechanical ventilation system may be required for structures built from more rigid materials. Such systems are often designed for year-round operation, and it is recommended to have a mechanical ventilation system.

Whatever greenhouse design you choose to create, it is important to understand proper ventilation. The growth of your plants will suffer without proper ventilation.

Humidity

Humidity here refers to the amount of moisture in the greenhouse growing environment. It is no news that keeping the wrong humidity in the greenhouse is detrimental to the growth of the plants. Here are a few tips on how to maintain the right relative humidity:

1. Avoid overwatering your growing medium. Too much watering is the beginning of trouble in the plants' root system. The humidity level in the greenhouse increases when there is too much water in the medium.

2. Ensure enough air circulation. This will improve the ventilation in the greenhouse and invariably ensure the right humidity level.

To keep plants from succumbing to disease, humidity must be kept in check. High humidity content in greenhouse air increases plant condensation, hampering breathing. Moreover, high humidity is a breeding ground for rodents and fungal diseases of plants. The vapor pressure deficit (VPD) must be routinely measured and maintained at the optimum level of 0 to 1 psi for better management of humidity. VPD is an ambient humidity measure as opposed to the humidity at which water condensation starts.

Shading

Shading is a temperature and light control device that uses shades or blinders that are automatically operated. The curtains close when there is too much sunshine during the day or when it is required to maintain warm temperatures at night in the greenhouse. An internal temperature sensor detects and triggers the opening or closing of the shades.

The sun in summer can really scorch your plants, especially in a greenhouse. It is advisable to have shades fitted to the outside that can be easily rolled into place as necessary.

Benches: Not only provide the extra spacing in which you need to work, but they can also prevent you from bending too much. Looking for a ventilated shelving system that provides good drainage of water and circulation of air is a good idea.

Specifically, lights are required to provide your plants with photosynthesis up to 24 hours a day. Now, what's a greenhouse point if you don't have the winter option to grow seasonal veggies? Look at the latest fluorescent light designs that have recently reached the famous HID lamps.

While it is smart for all greenhouses to employ screens or shade cloth to reduce the heating impact of sunlight, it is absolutely critical for a free standing greenhouse. A free standing greenhouse is usually a large structure, so it takes longer for the heat to build up to a damaging level. However, because it is so large and the air mass inside is so hard to move, it takes much longer to evacuate that heat to safe levels.

A shade cloth or screen will block a certain amount of light from entering. This limits catastrophic heating, while also protecting the leaves of tender seedling from sun scald.

Shade cloths come in different densities that block different amounts of light. A shade cloth with a 40 percent density, blocks 40 percent of the light. A shade cloth with a 60 percent density blocks 60 percent of the light. I personally prefer a white shade cloth with around a 40 percent density. If you are buying a free standing greenhouse as a kit from a greenhouse supply, they will usually recommend the correct shade cloth density needed for that particular design.

Shade Cloth is usually made of polyethylene covered by UV and helps with heating and condensation. They can all be cut to suit your greenhouse practice.

Min / Max Thermometers: Measure both indoor and outdoor highs and lows. But what's important about these thermometers is it will provide you with valuable information about how a given day's temperature fluctuates. This alone will tell you in your greenhouse if you need additional cooling or heating elements that can help you with your budget.

Watering systems have several different services, primarily to help with plant growth, cooling, and moisture. Depending on the type of greenhouse you want, you usually want to keep the humidity around 60%.

You might want to invest in these for a little more complicated greenhouses: when you're home, thermostats will support your greenhouse. Place a thermostat right in the middle of your greenhouse if you want to keep a worry-free temperature in your

Chapter 4 Start Growing In Your Greenhouse

One of the biggest benefits of a greenhouse is it gives you somewhere to start your seedlings off, so you get a head start on the growing season. I always used to start mine on windowsills, but my wife never appreciated me moving the ornaments and family photos to do so. Not to mention that the cats would sit on them, eat them or just knock them off and get soil on the carpet.

Even a small, plastic portable greenhouse out in your garden is sufficient to start your seeds off, and the extra warmth means you can get a really good head start on the year.

Germinating seeds is something many of us will do every year, but it is often touch and go as to whether or not they will germinate. It can be hard to find enough space to germinate all the seeds that you want to plant, and you end up not planting some crops you wanted to grow.

A greenhouse is a real boon because it gives you plenty of space to start your seeds in a protected environment.

You then need a decent growing medium. A good, peat based seed compost is a good place to start though you can mix up your own formulas. Avoid cheap compost because it tends to dry out very quickly, have large lumps in and not be as good for your seedlings. You can find your seeds rot before they germinate because the cheap compost doesn't drain well.

Seed trays and containers are good to get, and I often use ones with plastic lids. This way I can have a greenhouse within a greenhouse or I can use the plastic lid as I am hardening off the seedlings.

There are a huge variety of seed trays on the market, and I use a combination of open trays and trays with cells. Depending on what I am growing I will use different seed trays. Larger cell trays are used for larger plants whereas open trays are used for seeds that can be scattered like beetroot, carrot and so on.

For some seeds, such as sweetcorn cardboard tubes (such as those found inside toilet rolls) are good to use because the seedlings do not like being handled. The tubes can be planted straight in the ground, and the cardboard will rot as the seedling grows.

Larger plants such as squashes are best sown in individual pots so they can grow to a decent size without having to be re-potted, which they can object to.

You can use peat pots to grow your seedlings in though I have found these have a habit of either drying out too much or becoming sodden and then rotting. Some people like these but I'm not keen on them.

All of these can be sat in seed trays to make it easier for you to organize your plants. Just remember that you have to prick out your seedlings and re-pot them when they get to a certain size and certain types of plants will not appreciate this.

Heat mats can be used to help with germination, but they are not necessary. If you live in a really cold climate, then they are a benefit, but it does require that you have electricity in your greenhouse, which not everyone will have. You also have the expense of buying the heat mats so you may get one or two to start off your most important or delicate seedlings.

I have a hydroponic system with grow lamps at home which I use to start off seedlings like tomatoes and pumpkins. These are then transplanted to pots and put in the greenhouse where they continue to flourish.

You need to think about the light requirements of each plant because some seedlings prefer more light to others. More sun sensitive seedlings will need shading from the heat of the midday sun.

One useful technique when sowing seeds in individual pots is to place two or three seeds into each pot, spaced out evenly. This way if one or two seeds do not germinate you still have a third which could grow. If all three grow, then you can either prick out and re-plant the three seedlings, or you can discard the smaller seedlings, keeping the strongest.

All seeds need to be covered by the growing medium but not too deeply otherwise they will not push through the soil to the light.

Check the packets to determine exactly how deeply to plant each seed.

For bigger seeds, it is easy to poke them into the soil. One thing to remember with larger seeds such as squash seeds is to plant them on their sides so they can grow the right way up. If they are put in the ground the wrong way, then you can find the roots coming up through the soil and the leaves growing underground! This often happens when children help with the planting.

For smaller seeds, you need to cover them with a sprinkling of soil to stop them blowing away. With smaller seeds, you will need to be careful watering them as they can float away with excess water!

Seeds can take anything from a few days to a few weeks for them to germinate, depending on the type of plant you are growing. Check the packet for specific timings, so you know when to start checking your seedlings.

During this time, you need to keep them moist, but not wet otherwise the seeds can rot. Check the pots regularly and make sure they are not too damp. Peat pots can go moldy if the humidity is too high so you need to keep an eye on them too.

When you plant your seeds will depend on the type of plant you are growing. Check the instructions and plant during the time they state. Remember that with a greenhouse you can start your seedlings earlier in cooler areas than you can outside.

Hardening Off

Not all of your seedlings are going to spend their lives in your greenhouse; some will be planted outside. Moving a plant from the protective enclosure that is your greenhouse into the great outdoors can be an incredible shock to the system. The difference in environments causes shock which can at best stunt the growth of your plant by several weeks, and at worst kill it!

Hardening off your seedlings is vital if you want them to survive and thrive when you plant them outside of your greenhouse. You will be surprised how many people don't do this and struggle to get their plants to grow.

The process of hardening off isn't done overnight and can take a week or two, depending on the weather where you live. You will have to be patient, but it is worth it as it strengthens your plants and ensures they grow well.

Once there is no risk of frost during the day you take your seedlings out of your greenhouse and leave them outside during the day. Put them somewhere that is warm but not too sunny, and that is sheltered from the wind.

Leave your seedlings outside for most of the day and then mid to late afternoon move them back into your greenhouse.

Repeat this for two or three days and then gradually move them into sunnier locations and leave them out for longer.

After a couple of weeks, the seedlings should be in the location where they are to be planted and be left out all day and throughout the night.

Should your plants show any sign of stress such as browning, wilting or yellowing then move the hardening process back a step and try again the following day.

Water well during this process and then after the two weeks, you should be able to plant your seedlings out in the ground. It is worth keeping a close eye on them as some may benefit from horticultural fleece or a cloche if the weather starts to get cold or if there is a surprise frost.

Sorting Your Seed Packets

Most gardeners will have seeds packets pretty much everywhere, in drawers, on shelves, tucked away in cupboards. They accumulate, and it is far too easy to get overwhelmed by them. You know what it is like, you get halfway through the growing season and realize you forgot to plant something because you couldn't find the seeds!

There are plenty of different ways for you to organize your seed packets and it is up to you how best you do it. However, I would strongly recommend that you do organize them because it will make your life easier throughout the growing season and save you money from buying duplicate seed packets.

Firstly, I sort the seeds into three piles:

1) Herbs
2) Flowers
3) Vegetables

These are stored separately.

Each seed packet is filed under the first month in which it can be planted.

For me, this is the best way to organize my seeds because I know that in January I can look at my January seeds and decide what to plant (assuming I don't have a plan for the year). It makes my life much easier because I am not sorting through piles of seeds trying to work out what I should be planting.

This is my method and it works very well for me. It keeps me a little bit more organized and saves time when it comes to deciding what to plant. If you find a different system works for you, then by all means use that.

Remember that if a seed packet states it can be planted out in a month, then you can often start the seedling off in a greenhouse between four and eight weeks earlier, depending on whether it is heated or not!

A greenhouse is a real boon when it comes to starting off seedlings and will help you get a head start on the growing season. It also gets the seed trays out of the house and gives your plants a great start in life.

Many growers tend to ask the difference between vegetables, herbs, and fruits. A vegetable is a plant or any part of a plant that is considered edible and can be eaten. Herbs, on the other hand, refer to plants or part of plants that are grown as food and also for medicinal purpose while fruits are eatable products containing seeds which are formed from the matured ovary of a flowering plant. The major difference is that while fruits can be referred to as vegetables, vegetables cannot exactly be termed fruits. Also, it is arguable that not all herbs are eaten as the main ingredient as is the case of vegetables.

Growing Vegetables in a Greenhouse

Vegetables are suitable plants to cultivate in a greenhouse because the demand for them is usually high all through the year. However, the vegetables require the right environmental condition for successful cultivation. The grow lights in the greenhouse should be energy efficient and cover the vegetable plantation. During the cold season, the best vegetables to cultivate include; tomatoes, lettuce, spinach, peppers, and cucumbers. But with experience, any kind of vegetable can be successfully cultivated when provided with the right temperature. The key is to maintain a nighttime temperature between 40 – 62°F in the greenhouse depending on the type of vegetable. One of the major issues growers face when it comes to growing vegetables in a greenhouse is the issue of pollination. While some vegetables like tomatoes and peppers can self-pollinate, the others that cannot self-pollinate will require hand pollination. This is achieved by taking the anther of a vegetable and rubbing it carefully against the stigma of another vegetable for a successful transfer of pollen grains. Sometimes, the vegetables that can self-pollinate require being shaken in order to successfully pollinate but a circulation fan can be installed for this purpose.

Vegetables need water but not too much and so it is important not to overwater your greenhouse vegetable garden. A good ventilation system in place will maintain the proper humidity level which will aid the growth of the vegetables in the greenhouse. Using air conditioners in your greenhouse is not the best practice because what conditioners actually do is that they reduce the moisture content in the growing environment. It is advisable to use evaporative air coolers in the greenhouse instead.

Growing Fruits in a Greenhouse

The most popularly grown fruit in a greenhouse is tomatoes, but this does not mean that only tomatoes thrive in a greenhouse environment. All fruits including vines, peaches and even citrus fruits are suitable and can perfectly be grown in a greenhouse environment. Not all varieties of grapevines require high temperature for healthy growth, there are some varieties such as the black Hamburg that grow perfectly in a cool growing environment. The only thing about cultivating vines is that they are attention-demanding as they are susceptible to pest attacks and therefore should be closely monitored in order to ensure a perfect growing condition for them. As the grapevines grow, some maintenance practice needs to be carried out such as spur pruning, fertilization, etc. and waterlogged soil should also be avoided. Peaches and Nectarines are also very suitable for cultivation in a greenhouse but the right variety should be carefully selected. This is because some varieties of Peaches such as Hale's early require the presence of another variety nearby in order to carry out pollination successfully. A suitable variety of Nectarines for greenhouse cultivation is the Pineapple. Hand pollination can be done for the successful pollination of fruits that do not self-pollinate. It is also interesting to know that citrus fruits such as oranges and lemons can be successfully cultivated in the greenhouse.

Fruit and Vegetable Growing Calendar

Greenhouses are great for your summer crops and extending your growing season, but if they are heated, you can grow all year long. However, this isn't particularly cost effective as the cost of heating your greenhouse far outweighs the cost of buying the vegetables you can grow.

Saying that though, even an unheated greenhouse helps you to grow throughout the year and can be very cost effective indeed.

In late winter and early spring, you can start off hardy plants such as cabbage, leeks, lettuce, peas, onions, broad beans, Brussels sprouts and so on. These are then planted out once the weather warms up.

If you do heat your greenhouse, then plants such as tomatoes and peppers can be started off early too.

In mid-spring, your more tender plants are started off, such as pumpkins, zucchini (courgettes), squashes, sweetcorn, French beans and so on. This means that towards late spring they are ready to be planted outside or under glass. At this time of year, you can also buy ready grown pepper and tomato plants for your unheated greenhouse.

As spring progresses and summer begins you can plant your summer plants in their final locations in your greenhouse. Your outdoor crops are hardened off and planted out once the risk of frost has passed, which frees up space in your greenhouse.

If you have space in your greenhouse then towards the end of summer you can sow lettuces, salad leaves, and even baby carrots under glass for a later crop. You can also plant your Christmas potatoes in bags.

In winter time you can sow your broad beans and peas to overwinter before being planted out in spring. Calabrese and French beans can be planted and will mature in the greenhouse. Hardy lettuces will also grow happily in your greenhouse. You can also start any over-winter onions too.

Hardy plants such as kale and chard typically grow well outside during the colder months, but in some areas, they may benefit from being under glass during the extreme cold to ensure you get a good crop.

What you can grow throughout the year in your greenhouse will depend greatly on where in the world you live and how cold it gets. In colder areas with heavy snowfall plants which would be left outside over winter (kale, Brussels sprouts, etc.) will benefit from the protection of the greenhouse. If nothing else this will prevent the snow from damaging the plants.

In warmer areas, the greenhouse will let you start your plants off much earlier so you can make the most of the growing season.

Unless you are going to heat your greenhouse, you will not be able to get crops such as tomatoes, cucumbers, peppers and chilies during the winter months. Unfortunately, the cost of heating tends to be prohibitive.

Most greenhouse owners will usually only heat their greenhouse enough to prevent frost, which will damage their tender plants. If you grow rare or unusual plants that cannot tolerate colder temperatures, then heating becomes much more expensive but necessary.

The location of your greenhouse plays a big part in how much you need to heat your greenhouse and what you can grow over the winter months.

A greenhouse positioned in a sunny, sheltered area will obviously remain warmer than one, such as mine, which is located in the open. A lean-to greenhouse will be warmer because it benefits from the heat coming through the wall from the house behind.

When it comes to growing all year long, you can be creative. But with so many variables there are no hard and fast rules, so you will have to experiment, seeing what works best in your greenhouse in your area.

Chapter 5 Managing And Operating A Greenhouse

In order for your greenhouse to be at its best you will need to maintain it. This means that you will need to be able to do things such as water, ventilate, and protect your greenhouse from pests on a regular basis.

Clean Regularly

All properly maintained greenhouses need to be cleaned regularly. This means you need to look for and remove any sprouting weeds and other unwelcome growths from your greenhouse bins. These need to be removed on a regular basis.

You may want to even use a handheld vacuum cleaner as you clean out some of these areas just to make sure that they are made as fresh as possible when the time comes for you to begin planting and growing once again. You also need to clean out all growing containers with bleach so that you can get rid of any potentially harmful bacteria and other particles from dirt. To maintain your greenhouse, you need to clean it out regularly.

Maintain a Constant Temperature in Your Greenhouse

Keeping a steady temperature is one of the most crucial factors in ensuring proper maintenance of your greenhouse. To accomplish this, you can:

- Purchase and make use of readily available monitoring systems. The work of some operations is not limited to monitoring the internal temperature of the greenhouse, but also checks the moisture and acidity of your soil, which are also very important.

- Consider using an evaporative cooling system as this is very popular as it cools the air inside with water. It is evident that most plants grow well in a moist and humid environment; this makes it an ideal choice if you want to maintain a constant temperature. Having a proper cooling system is one of the best and affordable ways of maintaining a greenhouse.

- Ventilation is another crucial factor to consider. Given that greenhouses naturally trap heat from sunlight, the temperature may be drastically increased. And this can be avoided by having proper aeration. You might need to consider installing an air conditioning unit if opening windows and doors proved insufficient. Also, installing airflow fans will help improve circulation. Another good idea is having lots of vents in your greenhouse surroundings.

- Lighting is also an essential factor in maintaining a stable temperature inside the greenhouse. It is necessary when you're growing plants that aren't in season. Apart from light, you may also buy heaters. Some heaters are very easy to use as they are automatically regulated.

Without proper ventilation your greenhouse will get to humid and your greenhouse veggies are subject to rotting in the heat.

To counteract this your greenhouse needs to be ventilated in order get rid of excess heat and allow for the replacement of stagnant air with fresh air.

This means that you need to have proper ventilation shafts positioned throughout the greenhouse. You also need to have fans in place in order to better circulate air within the greenhouse. Keep everything ventilated and your greenhouse will soon be in good shape.

Maintaining humidity in a greenhouse

Do not apply excessive water on your plants. If you have puddles of water, the moisture tends to increase. Applying water directly to the soil (not to the leaves) will also help to reduce evaporation.

It goes without saying that your crops aren't going to grow without water. But even more than simply watering the plants, you need to make sure that you are watering them right. This means not watering them too much or too little. Too much water especially early on in the growing season can drown your seedlings and, in some cases, even push them right out of the soil. This is obviously a self-defeating action toward your greenhouse goals! You really don't want to flood your plants with too much water.

Also, you don't want to water your plants too little either since this will lead them to becoming liquid starved and drying out. The best way to water your plants is to gently sprinkle the water onto them in imitation of falling rain.

Because in the great outdoors after all, mother nature waters her plants by gently sending rain drops down upon them. She doesn't do it by roughly dumping buckets of water down on one individual plant all at once—its done gradually drop by drop.

So, having that said, it could help your plants growth tremendously to simply lightly sprinkle your water over your produce. Also make sure that you water with a solid routine. If for example, you can commit yourself to watering your crops once every morning—go ahead and water them in this fashion.

Maintaining a greenhouse in winter

If you don't buy the idea of high-end heating systems, then the following budget-friendly tips will be of help:

Use bubble wraps. You can purchase horticulture bubble wraps at a nursery. Just remember that the larger bubble holds more light than the smaller one. Also, remember to use thermostat. If your heater already has a thermostat, then that's a plus, since the heater can be set only when needed. By always checking, a good thermostat will help, you will be able to know when a heater is needed and when not. Therefore, it will save you money and resources.

Be sure to place your heater in the right spot, where it would work most effectively. As part of the greenhouse maintenance budget rules, it's best to put electric fan heaters in an open area of the structure. Most preferably, place them in the centre. If your greenhouse is larger, heating the entire area may be costly.

In this case, you may divide the structure into smaller spaces so you can decide what area to be heated.

Take Care of Pests

Bugs will always find their way in, and while it is not impossible to 100% eradicate all pests in your greenhouse, you can certainly keep the most harmful of them at bay. It doesn't take long for a few bugs to turn into an infestation. One of the best ways to curtail their growth is to use natural plants as repellants.

Yes, there are many plants such as marigolds and even sunflowers that can be used as a natural insect repellant. But if the bugs persist you may want to invest in fumigation. Just be sure to keep all people and pets away from the area when you decide to fumigate.

Chapter 6 Insect, Pest And Mite Management

Pest Control - Managing Pests

The term pest control often conjures up images of people using sprays filled with chemicals. You might think that using such methods is rather extreme. But if you spot your wonderful tomatoes surrounded by ants or your beautiful flowers suddenly attacked by flies, then you might think of drowning those creatures in pesticides.

However, what might sound like a frightening scenario can typically be solved by taking a few precautionary steps. If all else fails and you still would like to consider using sprays, then do not worry.

The thing about pesticides is that they have an instant (and noticeable) effect. You can see the number of pests on your plants reduced. Nevertheless, there are certain effects in the long term – such as depleting the health of your soil and slightly poisoning your water – that might prove disastrous for you in the future. You might have to change the soil entirely. If you are using a raised bed, then this might not be a problem. However, if you have decided to plant directly into the earth, then getting rid of all that pesticide residue is a strenuous process.

Here is another thing that you should keep in mind; sometimes, getting rid of the pests may not be necessary. If you have aphids roaming around on your plants, then see if you have helpful insects that dine on these aphids. In fact, certain farmers are known to let the pests live. This is because they usually have some form of predator that can take care of the pest problem. This has two beneficial results:

- You do not have to spend time (and money, in some situations) on pest control activities.

- You let someone (or something) else take care of the problem for you. A friend in need is a friend indeed. Even if that friend just happens to have four legs, wings, or antennae.

Another thing to keep in mind; your problem might not be related to pests. It is easy to think that certain creatures have wreaked havoc on your lovely garden. Actually, it is certainly tempting to think that way. However, in many cases, the situation might just be because of other factors. Is there enough moisture for the plants? Are strong winds causing harm to them? Was there heavy rainfall recently? Did it hail? Even water pollution could be another factor to consider. You see, all of these factors cause unnecessary stress on the plants, which further begins to attract the pests in your area. Trying to get to the root of the problem might help you effectively remove the pests without using any pest control techniques (including pesticides).

The idea behind evaluating your garden is to know what kind of problem you are dealing with. That may help you decide if you would like to head over to the next step, which is the integrated pest management, or 'IPM' for short, process.

In IPM, farmers and gardeners take gradually stronger steps to get rid of the pests in their garden. They start by working on the conditions that help the growth of the crops. Are these conditions beneficial? Do the crops have everything they need? Once they are able to work around these conditions, they seek to establish a level of damage they can accept. Once that is done, they move on to using methods that have minimal toxicity. If that does not work, they begin using toxic or invasive methods.

Join the Resistance!

The first thing that you should do is focus on creating pest resistance plants. You see, gardeners and farmers often work with a plethora of plants species. Some of these plants have some unique traits. One of those unique traits is the ability of the plant to have disease resistance. This means that the plant suffers minimal damage from a specific disease, similar to how the human immune system builds resistances against diseases.

Many of the modern plants have built resistance to many diseases that could cause considerable damage. What's more, you can find plants that also have resistance to certain insects. For example, you can find special types of squash that can keep away certain types of beetles. This might help you effectively find a solution against these pests without having to resort to other methods of pest control.

In fact, when you are purchasing plants, you might receive information about what pests those plants resist. After knowing what pests are common in your area, you can match the plant to that particular pest.

Inviting Less Pests

While you might be confident that you have taken all the precautionary steps to keep away pests, there might be certain reasons your garden is still attracting those nasty critters.

Plant Conditions

Make sure you have placed the plant in the right spot, based on how much water, sunlight, and essential nutrients that the plant may require. This is because stress begins to affect those plants that do not receive what they require. The stress in turn causes plants to release certain chemicals in the air, which are like beacons for all the pests in the area. Humans might deal with stress through many means. Plants however, do not have mechanisms to resist stress. They eventually begin to experience deteriorating health and finally succumb to the effects of pests. This does not mean that healthy plants cannot attract pests, but they are capable of surviving attacks when an unhealthy plant may not be able to.

Mixed Plants

Most insects have receptors that allow them to target their favorite plants. It is how bees can seek out nectar so easily. If you have the plants that insects are waiting to attack and you have done nothing to protect those plants, then you might as well schedule buffet hours for the insects! What you can do to avoid this situation is to plant your crops in small batches throughout your garden. Then you can add other plants into the mix (preferably those that have resistance against the pests in your area). This confuses the insects, tricking them into believing that perhaps your garden does not have the food they are looking for. Additionally, you might be able to avoid diseases from spreading when you mix plant breeds.

Timing

Certain pests often arrive during certain climates. This fact might give you an idea of the kind of threat you are dealing with. When plants are young, they do not have the strength to ward off pests effectively, which is why you can plant your crops early so that by the time pest climate arrives, your crops have strong tissues. In some cases, insects often leave eggs behind in gardens. When the larvae hatch, they find a ready source of food in the plants around them. For this reason, you could also plant your crops a few weeks after the larvae have hatched, allowing you to starve the pests before working on your garden.

Here is a pro tip: speak to farmers in your area about the emergence of pests. They have extensive knowledge about when these pests might come out during a particular season, allowing you to know how long to wait before planting your crops.

Crop Rotation

You can move around the crops to new locations in your greenhouse each year. This does not give pests a particular spot to target. Shifting locations confuses the pests, who might be used to finding plants in a specific spot of the garden. Certain insects often lay their eggs in one location when they realize that they know where they can find a ready supply of food. However, by moving your crops around, larvae that hatch might not find their food source. Before they can discover food, they might starve and you might be able to get rid of them without much effort. Do note that crop rotation is most commonly possible with annual plants, when they can be cycled year after year. Perennial plants are usually harvested after one year, so they cannot be quickly rotated. So make a note of this when you plan to change plant locations in your garden.

Go Easy on the Fertilizer

This might be a common mistake committed by beginners. Gardeners who are starting out might worry about the amount of fertilizer that they use. Many use too much to avoid using too little. Unfortunately, too much fertilizer can cause harm to plants, just the way too little can. In fact, you could say that increasing the amount of fertilizer to a plant is like giving steroids to them! For example, soil nutrients provide nitrogen to the plant. This is good in moderate quantities. By adding more fertilizer, you increase the supply of nitrogen. Providing excess amounts of nitrogen might cause rapid growth in plants. This causes them to end up being juicy. This might not sound all that bad. Who doesn't love juicy food? You and every other multi-legged creature will be waiting to get a bite out of those plants. Pests might become attracted to the unnatural growth, finding a rich source of food for them and their offspring.

Clean Up Other Materials

If you notice fallen leaves, fruits, or other objects in your garden that should not typically be there, then make sure you clear them out. These objects and debris might carry organisms and pests on them that could be transferred to your plants. This increases the chances of infecting your plants with diseases or sending pests into their midst. Once you have cleaned up, see if you can also cultivate the soil when you get the opportunity. This reveals any hidden pest eggs. Additionally, if there are any larvae, you might just let predators (or even the weather) get rid of them.

Make Friends With Creatures

I am not asking you to invite creatures into your house for tea and supper. What I mean is to allow the growth of certain organisms that could help you get rid of pests. For example, certain types of spiders leave your plants alone, but find abundant food in the pests that might live there. You can always encourage the growth of these pest-hunters, as you can call them.

Identifying Dangers

No matter how experienced you become at gardening, there is no avoiding pests. If you have a plant growing in your garden, chances are that there is a pest out there waiting to pounce upon it.

What you should do is try and identify these pests. If you step into your garden one day and notice a spider or a group of ants on your plants, it does not mean that they immediately should be classified as pests. They might just have wandered into your colorful ecosystem looking for food. Get in touch with local farmers or perform your own research into finding out what creatures you should recognize as a threat and what organisms are safe. This way, you leave out the creatures who can help you and target those whom you don't recall sending an invite to attend your garden.

The next thing you should do after identifying a pest is to assess your plant for damage. It is easy to enter panic mode because, let's face it, pests are generally disgusting and you never know if they have laid any eggs or not. Which is why you should take your time to check the plants for possible damage. Are the leaves affected, or do you notice problems on the entire plant? Do you spot any discoloration? If so, is this discoloration spreading all over the plant or just restricted to a specific area? Has this infection or attack affected nearby plants as well?

Then it is time to look at the plant more closely. Check those areas that you wouldn't usually, like the bottom of leaves or the area where leaves meet stems. What you are doing right now is looking for traces of eggs, small insects, or organisms. Check the way these organisms or eggs are clustered. Make sure you approach the plant with care. You might frighten off these pests. While that might sound like a solution, it only scares them away for a short duration before they return. During this process, you are simply trying to find a pattern to their movement and organization. Return at different times of the day and watch the pests. If you are lucky, you might catch them in action, which helps you gain a better understanding about them. As you are gaining more information about the pests, keep making notes. You might need them later on for reference.

Using the above information, you can find out how to get rid of the pests while dealing the least amount of damage to your plants.

Knowing How To Deal With Your Pest

Here is where the information you gathered comes into play. Without the information, you might think that you need to act quickly and get rid of the pests. Time to bring in the big guns! However, what you should be doing is analyzing the situation properly. Do you see pests restricted to a particular plant or spreading out in your garden? Even if these creatures are spread out, do you notice them in few numbers or do you see hundreds of them?

This process is known as establishing damage thresholds. It basically means that you are trying to measure the extent of pest growth in your garden before taking reactive measures.

If you have a small number of pests, then you can think about using one of the solutions provided below. However, if the pests have multiplied to a considerable amount, then it might be the time to introduce the big guns (and by that, I mean pesticides).

Choose Your Control Method

After getting the necessary information and concluding how severe the pest problem is, you can choose various control methods to deal with the problem.

Physical Control Methods

If pests are getting to your crops, then you could try physically keeping them away. There are a number of ways to do this. Here are a few:

Erecting Barriers

Call this your initial defense plan. By setting up barriers, you can prevent pests from actually reaching your plants. A good example could be a fence, which are great for keeping away rodents and animals such as cats (yes, our feline friends can be pests, too). To protect against birds, you could use bird netting. Wire meshes and other forms of netting may be able to protect your crops from flying insects. When you become aware of what insect or animal causes your garden a lot of distress, you can choose an appropriate physical barrier.

Getting Handy

Many farmers and gardeners simply choose to use their hands to pick away the pests, if those pests are large bugs and creatures such as snails. This is an inexpensive and a non-toxic method of getting rid of your creature problem. However, if you feel squeamish about working with your hands, there are many bug vacuums on the market to help you do the job.

Using Water

If you discover small creatures inhabiting your garden without your permission, then you can easily get rid of them with a spray or stream of water. Simply bring your hose to your plants, turn on the water and dislodge these nasty critters. In addition to removing pests, you end watering the plants as well. However, do make sure that you do not use a lot of water. You might end up drowning the plants.

Adding Repellants

You can also utilize certain substances that pests do not come close to. For your typical garden pests, you can make use of special oils or scents. Look for any repellant that matches the pest that is currently attacking your garden. Oh, and by the way, by repellant, I don't mean a bug repellant!

Creating Traps

Traps work well because they are unexpected. They are designed to either lure a creature towards it or catch them unaware. A common example is the spring loaded trap for catching mice.

There are numerous traps for different scenarios, such as glue traps, electronic traps, and more. Find the one that suits your needs.

Biological Control Methods

Under these control methods, you are using a living organism to take care of the more dangerous organisms in your garden. Typically, this would mean using creatures beneficial to your garden (as we had seen some examples earlier). However, in this case, we are also considering substances that have useful bacteria or fungi that we can apply on the plants. These substances have a repelling effect. They prevent the pest from approaching your plants.

▼

Chapter 7 Fertilizers And Agrochemicals

Fertilizing Your Indoor Garden

Human beings need to drink and eat. When we consider watering, it is clear that plants also need to drink lots of fluids. But as it so happens, plants also need to eat. Only they need their nutrients to come from the soil or a liquid fertilizer. The roots of your plants stretch out underneath the soil, spreading in order to seek out more food to provide all the nutrients that they need to keep growing nice and healthy. If you are raising your plants in the ground outdoors, then those roots can stretch a good distance and find lots of nutrients. But when you raise those same plants indoors, there is only so much space in each container that they can spread out, and there are only so many nutrients in the soil. To make certain your indoor plants eat their fill, you need to fertilize them on a regular basis.

Regardless of what potting soil you decide to use, your plants will suck it dry of nutrients in less than two months. When this happens, they will begin to starve. You can buy time in this process by adding a slow-release fertilizer or manure pellets (such as chicken) into the soil. However, these are only going to buy your plants a certain amount of breathing space. They won't be enough on their own to keep your plants from starving. For that, you are going to need to create a schedule to regularly feed your plants a liquid fertilizer. There are many liquid fertilizers available on the market that you can purchase, or you can make your own. We'll see how to make our own in a moment, but before we do, it is a good idea to understand what exactly a fertilizer is providing for your plants. By gaining a knowledge of this, you have the best possible understanding of what they require.

The majority of fertilizers available are primarily focused on providing three nutrients to your plants: nitrogen, phosphorus, and potassium, or NPK. I say the majority of fertilizers because there are a decent amount on the market those focuses on only one of these three nutrients rather than all three. You can also purchase these nutrients on their own in a solid form meant to be dissolved in water. However, if you are purchasing pre-made fertilizer for your indoor garden, then the best idea is to choose a fertilizer that has an NPK ratio with equal amounts of each nutrient. Of course, it is rare that it is always a one for one ratio, and so it is okay for the ratio to be a little uneven so long as the nutrients are present in approximately equal quantities. If you are growing fruit or plants that fruit such as strawberries, raspberries, tomatoes, or peppers, then you are going to want to use a fertilizer with a higher amount of potassium as this helps the plants to grow their fruits properly. When using a store-bought fertilizer, you should always follow the instructions on the package so that you avoid overfeeding. When you overfeed them, the pH level in the soil rises to high levels. If you bought soil testing kits or an electronic pH reader, then you should keep a close eye on the pH level.

Buying fertilizer can quickly become expensive if you have a large garden to maintain. One way around this rising cost is to make your own. But be aware that it is always a very smelly process! One way to quickly get yourself some fertilizer is to fill a bag up with compost and let it soak in water for ten days. On day ten, you add water to the mixture until the color changes from black to slightly gray like tea, at which point it is ready to use. Another simple fertilizer uses urine as the primary ingredient since it is sterile, has a decent amount of potassium, and a lot of nitrogen in it, plus it's very easy to acquire because you can use your own! Dilute one part urine with forty parts water, and you have yourself a quick and efficient fertilizer. However, although this method is a little more difficult, you may be interested in making a comfrey fertilizer due to its high potassium concentration. The same steps you take to make a comfrey fertilizer can be used to make a nettle or a borage fertilizer if you need a higher nitrogen count.

Comfrey is a herb from Europe that has high levels of potassium, phosphorus, and nitrogen. That means this one herb can provide you with all the NPK you need from a fertilizer. There are ways to turn this into a fine fertilizer, but it's necessary to note that what is really great about comfrey is that you can grow it yourself as a part of your herb garden so that you can always have plenty of source material to turn into fertilizer. It is pretty much one of the best investments you can make when it comes to feeding your plants. When there is too much carbon in a plant bed, this can make it hard for the plants to get the best benefits from the nitrogen in the soil. Comfrey has a carbon-nitrogen ratio that is perfect in preventing any of these issues.

To make fertilizer out of comfrey, all you need to do is stuff a bunch of comfrey leaves into a large container. Cut a little hole in the bottom of the container, and put a smaller bowl underneath to catch the black liquid that drips out. It takes a few weeks to start producing this black liquid, though it can be sped up by using a heavy object to press down on the leaves. This liquid is excellent for fertilizer when you mix it with water in a 15:1 ratio. That's all it takes to make comfrey fertilizer, but there is more you can do with comfrey around your garden. Take the leaves out after the pressing and use them to feed your potatoes or tomatoes as a nutritious mulch. As long as you let comfrey leaves wilt for a few days first, it can be used in this manner. You can also add comfrey leaves to the containers you are planning to use next to add more nutrients to the initial soil. Make sure you are using it with slightly older plants and not young seedlings as it can be too strong for them and lead to nutrient burn. Finally, you can add comfrey leaves to your compost to help make it more nutritious.

If you purchased your fertilizer, then it will have instructions on how often to use it, and you should always listen to these instructions. However, if you have created your own, then you are going to need to educate yourself on the needs of the particular plants you are looking to feed. Some, such as fruiting veggies like tomatoes or peppers, will benefit from a weekly feeding schedule. However, there are others, such as lettuce, which don't need a regular fertilizer feed. You should always research your plants before seeding them by either Googling the information or asking your local garden center employees. Also, you shouldn't try to give fertilizer to plants that are overly stressed out. While it may seem like a good idea to dose them with fertilizer to help them get better, it is actually much less stressful on the plant to be given clean water instead. You also won't need to use liquid fertilizer on your herbs, as they generally grow best by being light on nutrients.

The light source must be kept as low as possible in the early stages. When the light is too far away from the seeds, the stems reach to the sun and become vulnerable and delicate. The amount of light required every day varies, but the rule of thumb is 14-16 hours a day. Soil temperature is essential, not room temperature, and your seed packets should be kept as recommended. Most plants do best between 70-80 degrees, but the temperature of choice varies. Do your research before you start. Control the watering again. The soil should not be soggy. When the first seedling leaves begin to appear, properly called cotyledons, the plastic dome should be removed. You should start fertilizing when your baby plants grow their second set of leaves. Continue feeding once a week using a half-strength liquid plant starter fertilizer.

Making the Most of Compost

Your greenhouse will be in high demand for nutrient-dense dirt. Decent topsoil and quality compost will be your best tools in the greenhouse. But you'll be going through a lot. Your best bet will be to gather compost and reuse as much as possible. You can make your own by capturing any plant waste left over in your greenhouse after harvest.

There are several methods of generating compost, but the most effective for small-scale greenhouses is a compost bin. You can incorporate a simple compost bin into your construction by building it near your greenhouse, or you can purchase a small barrel-style composter.

The media for your compost is right in your own back yard. After harvest, be sure to save up your root stock, leafy plants, and wood chips if you have them. You'll want to make sure they are in equal portions and free from disease, insects, and harmful chemicals. By the time you are ready to plant, you can pull from your compost to refill your pots.

Compost also generates small amounts of heat as the material inside decomposes. If you are struggling to maintain adequate heat in your greenhouse during winter months, you may be able to add a compost bin inside to bump the temperature a little. If you struggle with excessive heat, be sure to keep your compost bins a fair distance away from your greenhouse.

Chapter 8 Hydroponics In A Greenhouse

Hydroponic Gardening

In greenhouses, hydroponic gardens are established. It is the mechanism by which plants are not grown in any substrate or soil with nutrients in the water. This process shows very high flowers, fruits, herbs, and vegetables. This is a very controlled gardening method, as everything from set-up to harvest is carefully planned. There is more than one way to do this form of Gardening, and one that you can choose depends not only on your budget but also on your greenhouse size and style.

Hydroponics System

A hydroponic system should be designed to meet plant-specific requirements with the most reliable and efficient nutrient delivery method(s) available. The three main plant-requirements a hydroponic system must meet are:

1) Provide roots with a fresh, well-balanced water and nutrient supply.

2) Maintain an optimal level of gas exchange between the roots and the nutrient solution.

3) In any case of pump failure or power outage, protect against root dehydration and immediate crop failure.

Whether active or passive, hydroponic systems can be. The active system includes a mechanical means of recirculating the nutrient solution, whereas a passive system relies on capillary action, absorption, and/or gravity force to replenish nutrient roots. And apart from being more efficient in all spheres, and therefore more productive, how easily they can be implemented in an automated greenhouse is a superb feature of active hydroponic systems. To deliver outstanding results, the automation system does not have to be complicated. Just as a fan can be connected to a thermostat to control temperature, a timer may be connected to a pump to supply the plants with nutrients as needed. If such a device is properly designed, a large reservoir of nutrients may feed the crop for weeks before a refill is required. In this scenario, the garden will continue to thrive indefinitely, as long as the system is reliable, without the need for continuous supervision.

To order for a hydroponic device to be deemed efficient, we need to ensure consistent fulfillment of the three main plant needs. Efficiency is just as critical because it will determine the operating expenses, and can in some situations, avoid the increasing world from being disturbed. By intelligent engineering, the easiest way to build a stable, efficient system is. Combined with hands-on training. Despite the feats of modern engineers, these days are quite incredible, complex problems are sometimes solved with even more complex solutions.

Experience has proven that simple solutions tend to be the most reliable. So following the old US military dictum, Keep It Simple

Silly (KISS), the hydroponic gardener can certainly help to achieve consistent, reliable results.

And now that we have a more comprehensive understanding of how a hydroponic system works, let's look at how some of the active hydroponic techniques currently in use today employ some of the same hundreds and even thousands of years ago garden techniques used. One of the earliest records of people who use hydroponics describes the Mexican Aztec floating gardens. Such parks, complete with water lilies and hyacinths, were designed close to natural ponds. In natural ponds, plants in a bioponic setting derive water and nutrients directly from the dam. Waste products from fish, birds, and other animals provide the bacteria in the sand and mud a rich mix of organic nutrients to grow on. Such microbes' excrements then provide the plants with the nutrients which they need to survive.

Freshwater, in the form of snow that falls from the sky, replenishes the water that is transpired by the plants and lost to evaporation. In the same way, the falling rain or running water created aeration and drainage in the ancient water field. When the rain stopped coming, or the water was running dry, such plants would stagnate and eventually dry up. Because of this, these early garden builders designed complex irrigation systems composed of troughs that could supply water where it was most needed, and sometimes over great distances.

The Do-It-Yourself Greenhouse

Consider building your own greenhouse, if you're really handy with a hammer and saw. By doing an internet search for "greenhouse ideas," you will find other plans on the internet. It's a job that will take two people a weekend or so to finish and can give you 10 or 20 years of service when using quality materials. If clarification or change is needed, the city that normally should ask the nearest neighbors if they disagree. For this intention, before breaking ground, I visited my neighbors to fill them in on my plans. I wound up with several more mouths to feed, so it goes without saying. They never knew I was going to feed them anyway. It's a hydroponic garden, after all!

New and innovative businesses, in their numbers, are catching on to the market demand for inexpensive greenhouses in a hobby-style way. One of those firms, RION, has built a clever line of prefabricated full-size greenhouses that UPS will carry. From what I have heard, many of their treated wood parts fasten together in a couple of hours. For just a little more than you'd spend on materials, timber, glazing, and hardware, in a fraction of the time you can get up and grow in one of those cool prefab homes, and never think about rotting wood and termites to boot.

Chapter 9 Making A Profit From Your Greenhouse

While greenhouse gardening is a practice common among home growers, it is a system of gardening that can be utilized commercially for profit-making. The first thing to do when considering being a commercial grower is to write out the plan, what to grow and the size of the greenhouse. It is important to plan because failure to plan may result in the loss of the entire plantation and consequently the loss of the investment made. The following tips are provided to give you insight on how to make enough profit from your greenhouse:

1. Choose the right plant to grow

The very first thing to do as a commercial greenhouse grower is to do good market research. Research about your interested niche, that is, the choice of plant you want to grow. Keep in mind that the right plant to grow for a profit in your greenhouse would be the plant with high market demand. This is because your level of profit is determined by the size of your market. You should, therefore, consider how big the market size is for your niche choice. As long as profit-making is the goal, a plant in high demand will definitely give high returns. This is a jackpot for commercial growers especially when the plants that have high market demand are also plants whose growth can be hastened in a greenhouse, for example, vegetables.

2. Take advantage of growing out of season plants

Another smart way of making a profit off of your greenhouse is to grow out of season plants. This is because almost all out of season plants that are made available have high market demand. And when a particular plant that is out of season is in high demand, it means the cost of purchasing the plant will increase and therefore your profit is maximized. When considering making a profit from your greenhouse, take the time to study the market trends and look out for plants in high demand and then take advantage of it by making it available when it's out of season.

3. Maximize your greenhouse garden space

This is simple logic, when you manage your greenhouse space well, you get to grow more plants and therefore, have more yields. You should, however, be careful enough not to choke up your plants in a quest to make profit because you might destroy your entire plants in the process. Just ensure to maintain sufficient space between your plants and avoid tools not needed in your greenhouse.

4. Limit Wholesale purchase

While it is good business to sell your products to wholesalers so as to sell faster, the result of doing that is that most times it shrinks your profit margin. What you can do to improve your profit margin is limit the amount of wholesale purchase you allow and engage in more retail sales. With this, you will get to sell your product for a higher price than the wholesalers would normally buy.

5. Reduce the cost of production

In order to make the best profit off your greenhouse, it is important to reduce how much is spent in its production. There are several types of greenhouses and the best one (cost-wise) for your size of plantation should be chosen. This will increase how much profit you make at the end of the growing season.

6. Take advantage of vertical gardening

Using a vertical gardening system in your greenhouse allows you to grow more plants within your greenhouse space. It is stress-free and gives enough room for good ventilation. This means that you do not have to worry about congestion in your greenhouse when you use a vertical gardening system. Remember that having enough room for ventilation in your greenhouse means that you do not have to spend much on heat reduction in your system.

7. Prepare your market

Sometimes, it is not enough to know that there is a high demand for the particular plant you are cultivating. This is because most of these people already have suppliers that supply them. It will be wise for you to do more than research about the market demand for the plant you are cultivating and take it a step further by linking yourself up with the right people. By 'the right people' I mean connecting with those in the same business as you. Go all out to nurseries, florists, and also farm stores to prepare your market before your harvesting period.

8. Ensure quality produce

Ensuring quality produce at the end of your growing season also determines how much profit you make. If what you produce is not good enough, it simply means you will not be able to sell it for a good price, and that is if at all you are able to sell it. You should, therefore, ensure that you provide the perfect condition for your greenhouse plants so that they can grow healthily and give a good yield at the end of the growing season. When you are sure of the quality of your product, you can then proudly sell them for a perfect price.

8. Build an online presence for your business

In this age we are in, I cannot stress enough how important online presence is for those who want to go big. Regardless of the size of your greenhouse, as long as you are a commercial grower, be smart enough to build an online presence for your business. This will expand your business in a way you are not prepared for. Strive to not keep your business only to your locality, sell your business digitally and invariably increase your profit.

It is not news that you can make a huge profit from your greenhouse gardening. It all comes down to choosing the right greenhouse system, growing the right plant, maintaining the perfect growing condition for healthy growth, and having a ready market for your product. With all these in place, you are as good as ready to start profit-making.

Chapter 10 Year-Round Growing

When you plant your plants in a greenhouse, you can allow them to give you harvest as often as you want to. Obviously, plants will only give you a harvest when they are ready to. However, with the process of growing your plants on a schedule, you can make sure that you have some sort of harvest coming in all year long. We will look into how this works and some tips and tricks to help you along the way.

First, let's look into why you would want to have a harvest all year long. If you have plants that can be harvested from all year long, you have fresh fruits and vegetables available to you every day of the year. If you grow enough plants, this could even replace your produce purchases at the grocery store. It will allow your family and yourself to be the healthiest versions of yourself that you can possibly be. It will give you something to look forward to each day, and it will allow you to continue to feel the success of growing in your greenhouse throughout every single season. Having a year-round harvest greenhouse can be a challenging process, and we will look into these struggles below along with the benefits—but it can be a great thing as well.

Next, let's look into how you can make this happen. How can you possibly have a greenhouse that has produce available to you every single day of the year? It sounds like something that would be fairly difficult. In reality, it is actually a simple process. It requires a lot of work and a lot of planning, but once you get that plan into action, I can be a simple thing to follow through with.

In order to learn about how you can make this happen, let us look into what we already know. We already know that you can plant in greenhouses all year long. We already know that you can keep your plants alive in your greenhouse all year long and that you do not need to keep planting new plants for each season. Your plants can stay alive. We know that this is possible through the use of heaters and adequate lighting through artificial sources when it is winter, and we know that this is possible through fans and vents when it's hot in the summer. When you have a greenhouse that is able to be used every season of the year, you can, of course, plant in every season of the year.

No, let's look into what we do not yet know. We do not yet know how you can have plants give you a crop all year long. Of course, you are not going to get a tomato plant to keep producing your tomatoes constantly day after day for years straight. Fruits and vegetables have growing seasons. They have seasons were they grow food and seasons were they prepare themselves to do so. You cannot make an apple tree have apples all year long. You cannot make an orange tree grow oranges all year long. The plants need to have their time to prepare themselves oh, they cannot have food on them every single day.

Because of this, there must be another way to allow you to gain a crop from your greenhouse every day of the year. This other way is by planting your plants on the schedule. When you plant a seed, you know when it will become mature by the number of days it provides you on the back of the packet. For example, if a tomato plant takes 120 days to reach maturity, this will be listed on the back of the seed packet. When you know how long it will take in order to produce fruit or vegetables, you will be able to count on that plant to produce a crop for you at that time. Because of this, you will then know if you plant a tomato plant that you will have tomatoes in 120 or so days. The same holds true for every type of plant. When you plant something, you should be able to tell how long it will take that seedling to turn into a plant that bears food.

Now, if you want to have every month of the year filled with these tomatoes, you will need to simply plan a harvest for each month of the year. In order to do this, you will need to pick out that month that you want the plan to be ready, and count back 120 days or however long it takes tomatoes to reach maturity. Once you count back these 120 days, you will find that the day that you need to plant your seed on. Columbus Day, you will probably want to plant many seeds. If you plant many seeds, you will have a better chance of getting at least some of them to survive. As we mentioned earlier in the book, not all seeds will turn into seedlings. Because of this, you will want to plant many seeds to ensure that you get some plants out of your effort.

After you have planted your seeds, go ahead and find the next date when you would like a new tomato harvest to happen and do the process all over again. If you want your hair was to happen once a month, you can simply plant the seeds on the first day of every month. Once you have gotten the pattern started, the math will always be 30 days later. Because of this, you can simply plant on one day of the month every month.

If you plant one day of the month every month for a year, you should then have a harvest coming in every single day of the year. As long as you care for your plants in a way that allows them to bear fruit and vegetables, will have your plants set up on a staggering schedule to give you a crop.

You can choose to do this year-round growing with one type of plant or with all of your plants. If you only want carrots year round, for example, you could simply just choose to keep planting carrot seeds when you want them to grow. If you want all of your plants to have a harvest every day of the year, you will do this with all of your plants. Obviously, to do this, you might need a bigger greenhouse. If you only have a small greenhouse, you can consider only doing year-round growing with your favorite plants.

Another important factor to consider when growing plants all your robes is that your females need to be ready for every season. If you live in a cold area, you will want to make sure that your greenhouse is winterized and ready for the cold winter. You will want to make sure that your heater is working and that it is running, as well as that all cracks and holes that could be in your greenhouse are covered and are not letting air in. He will also want to make sure that any big jobs are done before winter comes so that you do not have to open the doors or windows for long amounts of time as this can make the air in the greenhouse become very cold very quickly. If you are growing your round and you live in a place that has very hot summers, you may want to be prepared with things like some shades and vents on your greenhouse for air circulation. For the spring and fall, you need to be prepared as well. The preparation for these seasons varies based on where you live—but for the fall, you should basically be prepared for winter; and for the spring, you should be basically prepared for summer.

Why do you need to have your greenhouse ready for every season? You need to have your greenhouse ready for every season because you are growing in every season. If you have a harvest every day, that means you are growing every day. This means that your plants need to be alive and healthy every day. In order to make this happen, your greenhouse needs to be repaired and in the optimal environment for the health of your plants as well as their success every day of the year. This means that you need to take your seasonal preparation and care very seriously. It has a much more detailed approach to this information.

Another thing to consider when you look into year-round growing is that you need to be ready to do a lot of work every single day of the year. When you do year-round growing, you do not have an off-season. You do not have a break in between crops where you do not need to go out into your greenhouse. You do not have a time where you are not doing multiple jobs at once, actually. You are actually growing seedlings, planting seeds, caring for plants, and harvesting all in the same day. This means that you are around growing can take a lot of your time and energy in ways that typical greenhouse gardening cannot. Of course, for this extra effort, it does provide a lot of added benefits with its increased amount of crop and harvest, but it neh to be a level of work that you are ready for if it is something that you want to consider. This extra work also takes up a lot of extra time. If you want to have a year-round growing garden inside of your greenhouse, you need to make sure that you have enough time to do so. Finding the time to prep for each season, plant seeds, care for your plants, and harvest all at the same time can be really challenging. Year-round growing of your friend house is a commitment that you really need to be all in for if you want even to consider it.

With extra harvests, year-round growing also comes with extra costs. If you want to grow plants year-round, you will be buying many more seeds. You will also be buying much more soil, and maybe even many more trays if you cannot reuse the old ones. You will be using more water well water in your extra plants, and he will be using more light to provide the heat and lighting that your extra plants need. Make sure that you are able to cover these extra costs if you are ready to have extra harvests year-round growing in your greenhouse.

Another thing that you should know about year-round gardening is it is great for people who want to sell their crops. If you are looking to sell fruits or vegetables, year-round gardening can be a great choice. If you do your own gardening and sell your crops, you will be one of the few farmers or gardeners who are able to sell fruits and vegetables during their offseason. If you can sell fruits and vegetables during their offseason, you will have a huge advantage over your competition. Typically, people really miss fresh fruits and vegetables in the winter time. If you are able to provide them with you is, you will have a lot of business. You will have a lot of happy customers, and the extra work that you put into your year-round gardening will pay off quickly.

Year-round growing can be hard. Because of this, we want to share with you some piece of advice. Let's look into some tips and tricks that you can use to make year-round growing easier for you. Our first step is that you should start with a plant. Make sure that you know what you want to do. If you do not have a plan in place before you begin, you are around growing can seem really overwhelming. You need to know what types of plants you want to have and when you want to harvest them. You also want to have a plan for where you are going to grow your plants since they take up extra space as well as how you are going to get the extra resources. You may even want to plan out how you are going to have enough time to spend growing all of these plants at once.

Our next tip is that you should make sure you have a large greenhouse for a creative space plan before planning on having a year-round harvest. It is okay if you have a small greenhouse, but if you do have a small greenhouse, you need to be creative with the small space that you have. Look into different shelving units, or even considered growing one set the plants underneath the normal bench with artificial grow lights in order to maximize your space.

Also, if you are planning on participating in year-round growing, consider asking for help. Ask your friends and family to help you with watering once in a while. Ask your neighborhood children to help you with planting seeds. These are things that your family, friends, and neighbors would probably love to help you with if you asked him. The extra help would also give you the ability to care for plants in a way that you may not be able to do on your own.

Along with that last tip, if you offer some of the harvests to your helpers, they may be much more willing to help. Tell your neighbors that they can take some tomatoes whenever they like if they come over and help water them or help you plant some seeds. If you spread the word that you are helpers will get it back in produce that comes from your garden, you will probably have many more volunteers as well as much better luck getting them actually to come and help.

Our biggest tip for year-round growing is to be prepared. Look ahead at the challenges that you might face. Be ready for what you need to do if you have some sort of greenhouse emergency. Make sure that you understand you will be using many more lights and much more water. Understand that you will be

In many sizes and forms, greenhouses come. Each is unique in its own way and is suitable for the kind of plants you wish to grow. There are those designed for beginners and those made for the professional gardener. Whatever you choose will decide what you plan to grow and how you use a greenhouse will ultimately determine your buying.

If you're one, you will want a robust greenhouse. You certainly don't want to fly through the yard with high winds in the first storm. Make sure you select a reputable dealer and search in your greenhouse for some standard construction designs.

Make sure the greenhouse you choose has a lot of ventilation windows and is made long-lasting. You can usually choose models that are more inexpensive manually, or you can choose models that move up and down the house windows. All ventilation windows must have screen to avoid insects attacking you and your plants during the warm months.

A portable greenhouse may be of interest to you. It's great for children who are interested in planting and watching things grow. This is also a good choice for people who rent their homes. When you pass, your greenhouse will easily be packed to go with you. The portable greenhouses are as effective as any other kind of greenhouse effect.

Were you aware that you could garden in your high-rise apartment on the veranda? If you want a lawn, but you felt you couldn't because you live in an apartment in town, you're in to have a treat. The indoor greenhouses are available to you. Both models are smaller than the larger ones and serve almost the same function and operate very well. These are great for the smaller courtyard gardens.

There are a couple of things you need to know about home greenhouses. You will need to learn a few supplies to grow in a greenhouse. It's kind of like setting up house furniture. The first thing you will need for a new greenhouse is a table for plants. You will use any of the outdoor table, or you can choose one provided by your greenhouse dealer.

Pots and flats holding your plants can be found in any kindergarten. Most of the plants you buy already come with your own. However, you will need all the supplies necessary if you are to start plants from seed.

Combine a range of a number of potting soils. You will also need other forms of fertilizer the plants you expect to grow. You can get tips on this in your local kindergarten or online.

The tools you need to learn about greenhouses will be relevant. You will need a number of small shovels and truffles in a greenhouse for your gardening activities. You'll also need gloves. Many soils and fertilizers can be pleasant on your skin, and some flowering plants such as roses do not have thorns.

Don't forget that you're going to need a greenhouse heater when it gets old outside. An outdoor greenhouse can be gardened throughout the year. A variety of heater models are available, which are only designed to heat a greenhouse. Normally, you will buy them for the same dealer you purchased your greenhouse.

There is a method available called hydroponics to those of you who know a bit about gardening in a greenhouse or even to those who still learn all about home greenhouses. This is a kind of cultivation that allows plants to grow like minerals and supplements in just water. No soil is used in a hydroponic cultivation process. This is a very popular way of growing plants in a greenhouse and was found to make crops like tomatoes and peppers very effective.

There is a lot to learn about home greenhouses, and you will learn much when you work one yard. The fun of a greenhouse is to experiment and learn what you can and cannot grow.

Printed in Poland
by Amazon Fulfillment
Poland Sp. z o.o., Wrocław

mildew, molds, discoloration, wilting branches, rotting fruit - all of these are signs that your plants have caught a disease. The first step in tackling most sicknesses is to cut away any infected parts and immediately dispose of them outdoors. Apply treatments to your plants after ensuring those treatments aren't harmful to humans.

There are several key steps you should take to avoid disease in the first place,. Apply neem oil on a weekly basis, even if there are no signs of infestation or infection. This is a preventative measure so that you won't have to deal with these annoyances. Also, keep a close eye on how much water and light the plants are getting to ensure that they aren't getting too little or too much. Next, check the pH level of the soil to make sure that they have enough nutrients, as too few can leave them sickly, and too many can cause nutrient burn. Finally, though just as importantly, make sure that dead plant matter is removed from the area. The compost that is used in the soil is fine, but leaves or branches that have fallen off the plants and are rotting in the general area are quite harmful. This rotting plant matter, when it isn't being used as part of a properly planned feeding system, can introduce harmful bacteria to your growing area. Always make sure you remove any dead or fallen plant matter from the growing area and wash your hands first before you start handling your plants.

Conclusion

Gardening is one of the calmest and most calming hobbies. Most people work in their gardens and flowerbeds for hours. The greenhouse is one of the easiest ways to enjoy gardening. You will deal with your plants throughout the year with a greenhouse. Read about home greenhouses and how in your gardening you can get the most from them.

Which will you need in your backyard for a greenhouse? It will rely on what you expect to expand and how much you are prepared to spend. You get some very cheap greenhouse kits while you also have a greenhouse installed to your specifications and pay for it a little more.

Where should you start learning everything about home greenhouses? The first place to look is on the Internet. There are many websites dedicated to greenhouse planting, while some are specialized in greenhouses. This way, you will find plenty of details or visit a kindergarten that sells greenhouses.

There are different kinds of greenhouses available for your home. A greenhouse kit is available. If you just start in your greenhouse hobby, this is a good way to go. These are also available online. You will be able to build your own greenhouse and learn all about home greenhouses with these kits. You can get a pack for it, no matter what size you choose.

Chapter 11 Planting in Warm and Cold Weather

Cold Weather

One of the main reasons why people create greenhouses is because it allows them to plant all year round. To be more specific, they are preparing for the colder months of fall and winter. While having a greenhouse will provide you the opportunity to grow the so-called winter plants effectively, it is no guarantee that you'll be able to raise them well. You'll still need to equip yourself with the right techniques for raising plants in cold weather. Here are some tips that can help you get by, as well as some plants that are best suited for such weather conditions.

Growing cold weather plants during the winter seasons allow you to make very minimal adjustments to the conditions inside your greenhouse. Often times, the minimal amount of sunlight received during these cold periods is more than enough to provide heat sufficient enough for these plants to survive. In fact, subjecting them to summer-type temperatures can prove detrimental for their growth. Another advantage of planting cold weather plants during this season is the fact that they can withstand even occasional freezing temperatures.

There is a huge variety of plants that can be considered at home with cold weather. You can grow these plants on low-temperature, low-light conditions without encountering too spending a lot of time in the greenhouse. Make yourself comfortable with these facts and even happy with them. If you do these things, it will be much easier for you to grow your plants year-round in a greenhouse.

Even though growing plants year-round in a greenhouse is hard, we want you to find success. We believe that if you follow these tips and tricks and learn all the information that we have shared with you, you will be able to have success at year-round gardening. As long as you have the tools, knowledge, and passion necessary to do this large task, you will have great success.

Overall, it is easy to see that year-round growing inside of a greenhouse is a difficult but rewarding task. It is something that takes extra time, extra money, extra resources, extra effort, and extra dedication in order to keep up with. Along with all of these things, however, year-round growing in a greenhouse also provides you with added benefits. It gives you harvests year-round. It allows you to have healthy food to put on your table every day of the year. It allows you to plan for what you want to eat and when you want to have it ready. It is a rewarding and beneficial process in many ways. Year-round growing can be a great thing to do—you just need to make sure that you are up for the challenge before you begin.